TO: _____

FROM: _____

DATE: _____

Majestic Expressions
Savage, Minnesota, USA

Majestic Expressions is an imprint of BroadStreet Publishing Group, LLC.
Broadstreetpublishing.com

When God Thinks of You He Smiles

© 2024 by BroadStreet Publishing®

9781424565764

All rights reserved. No part of this publication may be reproduced, distributed, or transmitted in any form or by any means, including photocopying, recording, or other electronic or mechanical methods, without the prior written permission of the publisher, except in the case of brief quotations embodied in critical reviews and certain other noncommercial uses permitted by copyright law.

Scripture quotations marked NIV are taken from the Holy Bible, New International Version®, NIV®. Copyright © 1973, 1978, 1984, 2011 by Biblica, Inc.™ Used by permission of Zondervan. All rights reserved worldwide. www.zondervan.com. The "NIV" and "New International Version" are trademarks registered in the United States Patent and Trademark Office by Biblica, Inc.™ Scripture quotations marked NLT are taken from the Holy Bible, New Living Translation, copyright ©1996, 2004, 2015 by Tyndale House Foundation. Used by permission of Tyndale House Publishers, Carol Stream, Illinois 60188. All rights reserved. Scripture quotations marked ESV are taken from the ESV® Bible (The Holy Bible, English Standard Version®), Copyright © 2001 by Crossway, a publishing ministry of Good News Publishers. Used by permission. All rights reserved. Scripture quotations marked CSB are taken from the Christian Standard Bible®, Copyright © 2017 by Holman Bible Publishers. Used by permission. Christian Standard Bible® and CSB® are federally registered trademarks of Holman Bible Publishers. Scripture quotations marked NASB are taken from the New American Standard Bible, Copyright 2020 by The Lockman Foundation. Used by permission. All rights reserved. Scripture quotations marked NCV are taken from the New Century Version®. Copyright © 2005 by Thomas Nelson. Used by permission. All rights reserved.

Typesetting and design by Garborg Design Works | garborgdesign.com
Compiled and edited by Michelle Winger | literallyprecise.com

Printed in China.

24 25 26 27 28 29 30   7 6 5 4 3 2 1

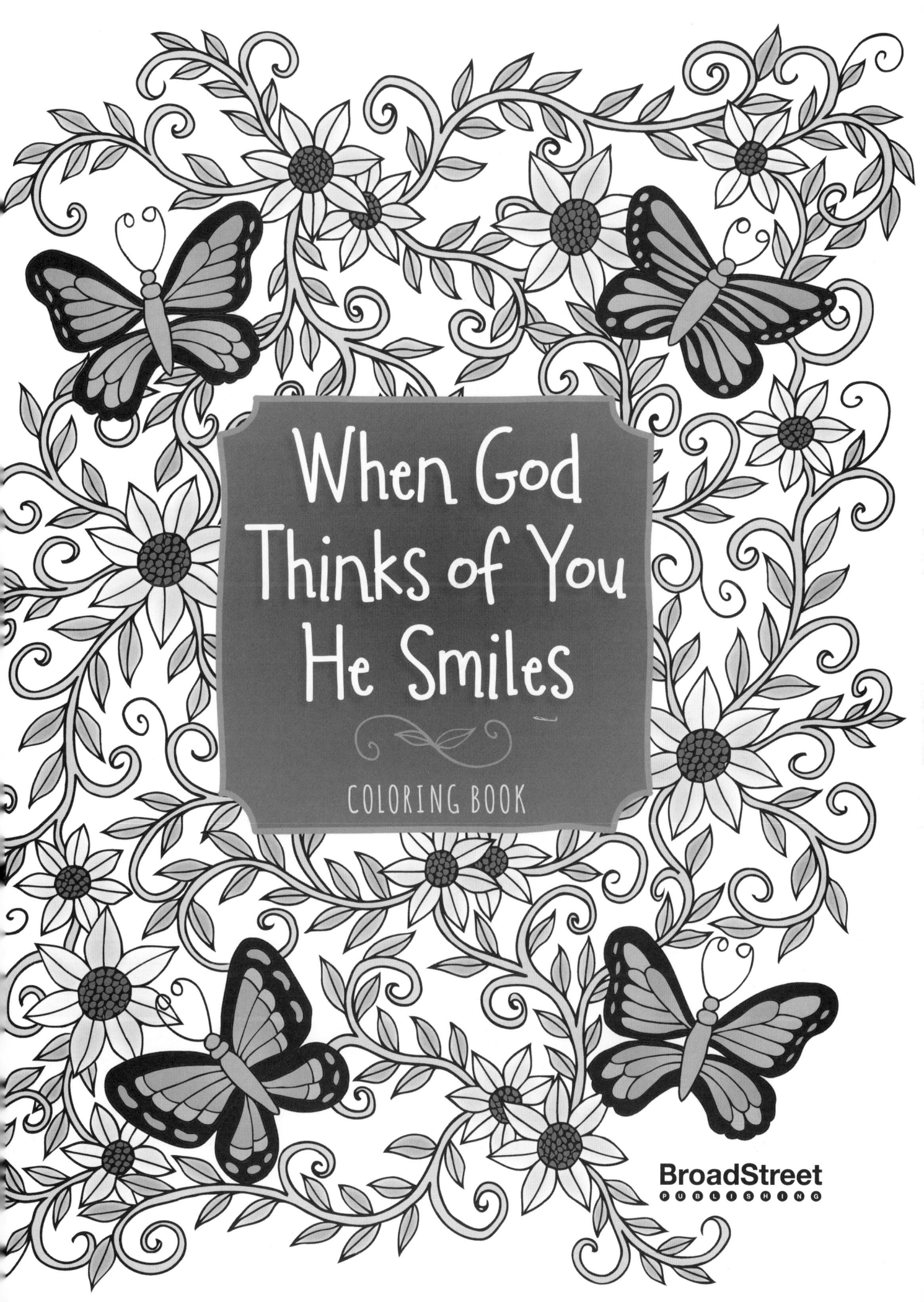

God so loved the world that he gave his one and only Son.

JOHN 3:16 NIV

He delights in people who are trustworthy.

PROVERBS 12:22 NIV

If anyone loves me,

he will keep my word.

JOHN 14:23 CSB

The Spirit produces
the fruit of love, joy,
peace, patience, kindness,
goodness, faithfulness,
gentleness, self-control.

GALATIANS 5:22-23 NCV

I no longer live, but Christ lives in me.
GALATIANS 2:20 CSB

For the joy set before him he endured the cross.

HEBREWS 12:2 NIV

You make known to me the path of life; in your presence there is fullness of joy.

PSALM 16:11 ESV

Welcome one another as Christ has welcomed you.
ROMANS 15:7 ESV

ROMANS 6:23 NLT

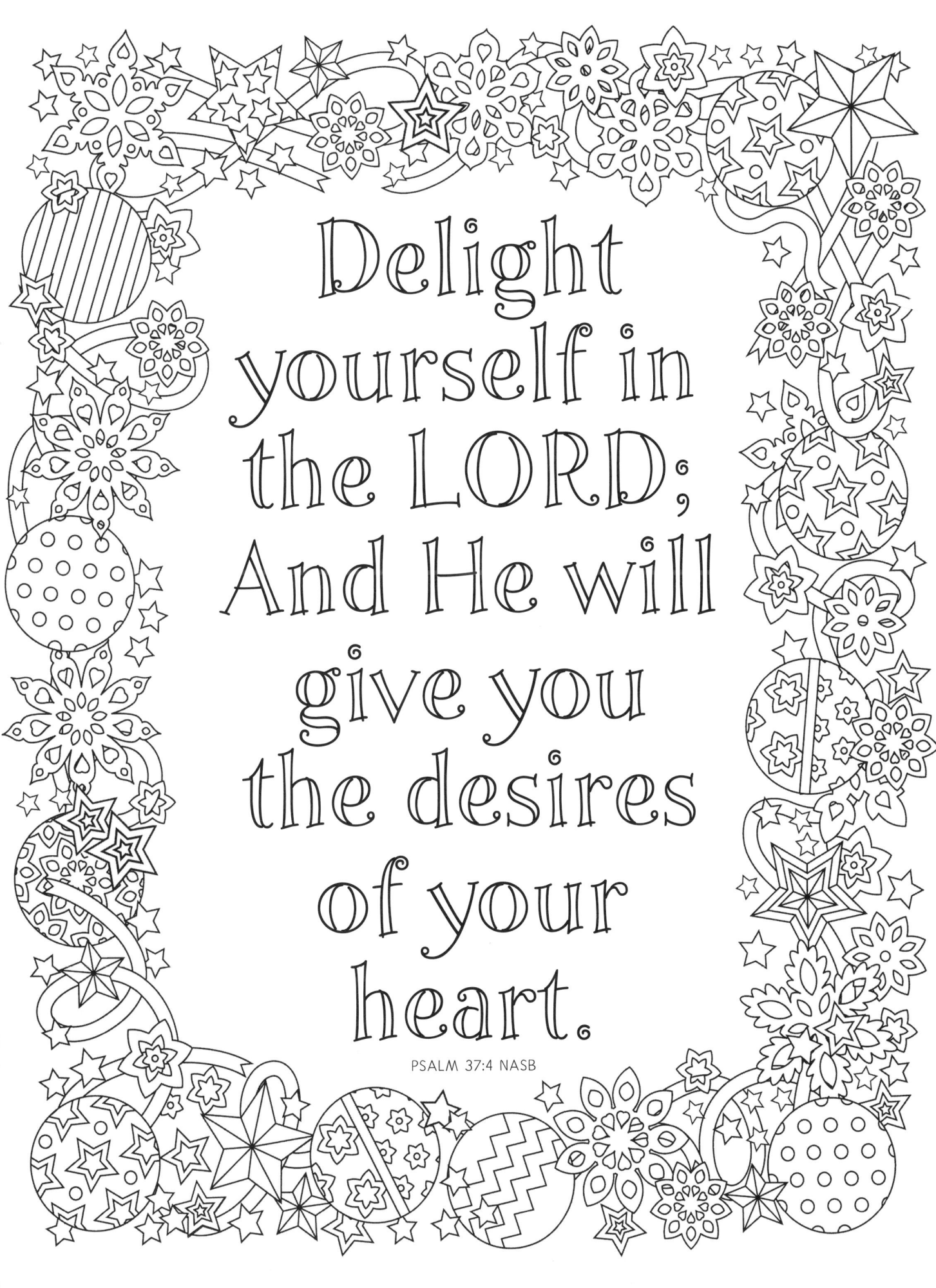

The mountains may move and the hills disappear, but even then my faithful love for you will remain.

ISAIAH 54:10 NLT

I PRAISE YOU
because I am fearfully and wonderfully made.

PSALM 139:14 NIV

The LORD looks at the heart.

1 SAMUEL 16:7 NASB

Every one of them will come to me, and I will always accept them.

JOHN 6:37 NCV

ASK,
and you will receive, that your joy may be full.

JOHN 16:24 ESV

I HAVE TOLD YOU THESE THINGS SO THAT YOU WILL BE FILLED WITH MY JOY.

JOHN 15:11 NLT